GEOGRAPHY MATTERS IN
ANCIENT ROME

Melanie Waldron

heinemann
raintree

Edited by Helen Cox Cannons and Jennifer Besel
Designed by Philippa Jenkins
Original illustrations © Capstone Global Library Limited 2015
Illustrated by HL Studios, Witney, Oxon
Picture research by Jo Miller and Pam Mitsakos
Production by Helen McCreath
Originated by Capstone Global Library Ltd

Library of Congress Cataloging-in-Publication Data
Waldron, Melanie.
  Geography matters in ancient Rome / Melanie Waldron.
     pages cm.—(Geography matters in ancient civilizations)
  Includes bibliographical references and index.
  ISBN 978-1-4846-0964-4 (hb)—ISBN 978-1-4846-0969-9 (pb)—ISBN 978-1-4846-0979-8 (ebook) 1. Rome—Historical geography—Juvenile literature. 2. Human geography—Rome—Juvenile literature. 3. Rome—Civilization—Juvenile literature. I. Title.

  DG30.W35 2015
  937'.06—dc23   2014013385

This book has been officially leveled by using the F&P Text Level Gradient™ Leveling System.

Acknowledgments
We would like to thank the following for permission to reproduce photographs: Alamy: © David Kilpatrick, 16; AP Images: PA Wire/Tim Ireland, 32; Bridgeman Images: © Look and Learn, 9; Corbis: © Atlantide Phototrave/Stefano Amantini, 15, Arcaid/© English Heritage, 29, Hoberman Collection, 36, Robert Harding World Imagery/© Godong, 37, © Bettmann/Philip Gendreau, 40, © Stapleton Collection/Philip Spruyt, 30; Dreamstime: © Smilemf, 4; Getty Images: De Agostini/DEA/R. BAZZANO, 8, De Agostini/DEA/DEA/A. DAGLI ORTI, 33, Hulton Archive/Print Collector, 39, De Agostini/DEA, G. WRIGHT, 13; Newscom: akg-images, 17; Shutterstock: Accord, 27, antb, 21, AridOcean, relief map (throughout), Andrew Bzh, cover, Claudio Divizia, 10, E.O., 24, Filip Fuxa, 41, Duncan Gilbert, 12, laraslk, 23, Fedor Selivanov, 34, Pavlov Valeriy, 35, SF photo, 5; Superstock: LatitudeStock/Capture Ltd, 25; Wikimedia: 28. Design Elements: Nova Development Corporation, clip art (throughout).

We would like to thank Brian Williams for his invaluable help in the preparation of this book.

Every effort has been made to contact copyright holders of material reproduced in this book. Any omissions will be rectified in subsequent printings if notice is given to the publisher.

Contents

Some words are shown in bold, **like this**. You can find out what they mean by looking in the glossary.

Who Were the Romans?

The Romans created a huge **empire** that spread across much of Europe, northern Africa, and eastern Asia. The Roman Empire lasted about 500 years. During that time, Roman building methods changed the towns and cities in the empire, and strong leaders ran the empire in a highly organized way. The enormous size of the empire meant that it included areas with very different **climates** and geography.

Romans were excellent engineers and builders. In all the parts of their empire, they set about changing the landscape. They did this by building things such as cities, **ports**, roads, walls, and bridges.

The Romans built fabulous buildings, like this one—the Roman Forum in Rome—in towns and cities across their huge empire.

The city of Rome grew up on the banks of the Tiber River.

Where did Rome begin?

Over 3,000 years ago, people settled on the flat land in the **valley** of the Tiber River. This is around halfway down the length of modern Italy. Villages began to grow on the seven hilltops around the valley. As the population increased, these villages grew bigger. Eventually, they merged together to become the city of Rome, in around 750 BCE.

The area was a good site to settle in. The flat land in the valley was **fertile**, so people grew crops and raised animals. The climate was not too hot or too cold, and the Tiber River provided water. The river was narrow at this point, and it also had an island in the middle, making it easier to cross. The site was 15 miles (25 kilometers) from the coast, so it was close enough to reach the open sea, down the river. The seven hills also gave good viewpoints for spotting any attackers.

How Did the Roman Empire Start?

The Roman Empire started in 27 BCE, when Augustus Caesar became the first **emperor** of Rome. The emperor was the supreme ruler. By this time, Rome had already taken control of lots of land outside of Italy. Italy had sea on three sides, so Romans could travel to many places by ship. They could journey by land northward into central Europe, although the Alps mountains were a barrier to travel.

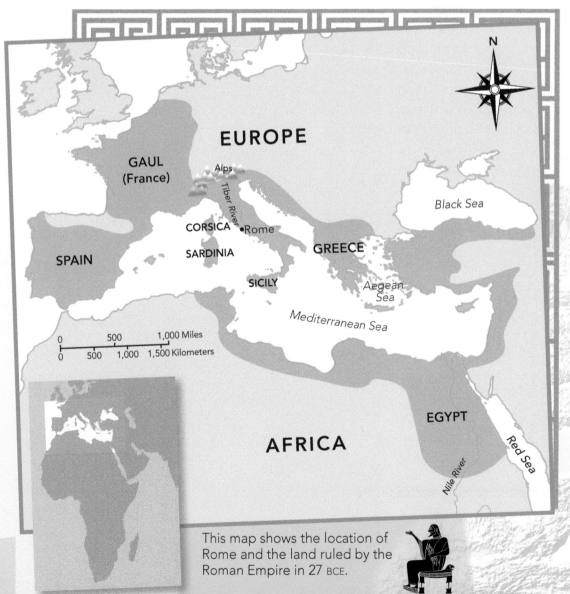

EUROPE

GAUL (France)

Alps

Tiber River

Black Sea

CORSICA •Rome

SPAIN

SARDINIA

GREECE

SICILY

Aegean Sea

Mediterranean Sea

0   500   1,000 Miles
0   500   1,000   1,500 Kilometers

EGYPT

AFRICA

Nile River

Red Sea

This map shows the location of Rome and the land ruled by the Roman Empire in 27 BCE.

Where was the early Roman Empire?

When Augustus Caesar became emperor, the lands of the Roman Empire included almost all of the coast of the Mediterranean Sea. Rome also controlled most of Spain, France, and Greece and the islands of Sicily, Sardinia and Corsica. Rome was located at the center of all this land.

What kind of landscapes were in the Roman Empire?

There were many different landscapes in the Roman Empire in 27 BCE. Italy had mountains, valleys, and flat **plains**. The snow and rain in the mountains provided water for Italy's rivers. The valleys and flat plains were good for farming. In northern Africa, Romans found valuable **minerals** in the hot, dry deserts. They also found good farmland along the Nile River. To the east, in Greece, the land was mountainous, and there were also over 1,400 islands in the Aegean Sea. Further east of this, the Romans came across more desert land, mountains, forest, and the coast of the Black Sea, in Turkey.

RED MARBLE

Romans found a source of beautiful red **marble** in Egypt's eastern desert. They used this in their most important buildings. The marble quarry was high up a desert mountain, and the Romans had to carry it across the desert for 200 miles (322 kilometers), to the Nile River. It could then be taken by boat to where it was needed.

How big did the Roman Empire become?

Under the emperors, the area of land ruled by the Romans grew. By 117 CE, the empire had reached its biggest size. It was around 2,500 miles (4,000 kilometers) from east to west, and around 2,300 miles (3,700 kilometers) from north to south. Over 50 million people lived in the empire, and all of the Mediterranean coast was part of the empire.

This is a section of a map that was drawn in the 13th century, as a copy of a 4th-century Roman map. It shows roads leading from Rome to all the parts of the Roman Empire.

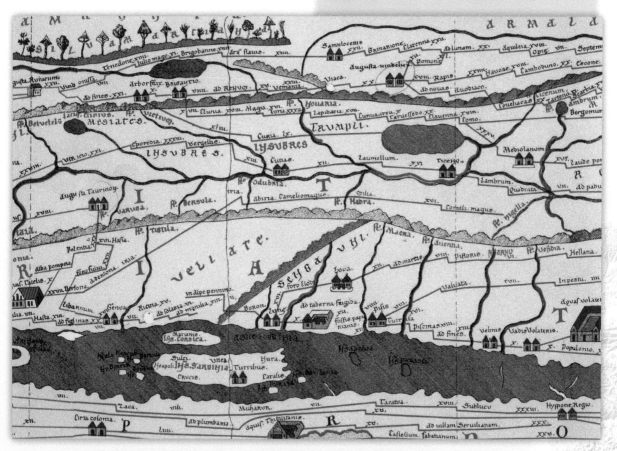

How did the Roman Empire expand?

The empire was able to become so big because of the strength of the Roman army. They were experts at building roads and bridges, so groups of soldiers could quickly march to places. Surveyors planned the routes that the roads would take and mapped them out for the soldiers to follow.

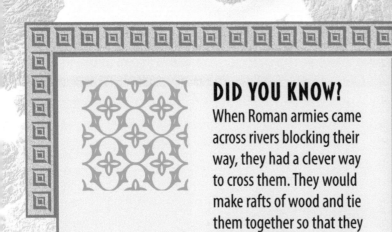

DID YOU KNOW?

When Roman armies came across rivers blocking their way, they had a clever way to cross them. They would make rafts of wood and tie them together so that they reached all the way across, like a floating bridge.

How did armies move so quickly?

Roman army leaders trained their soldiers to march at a quick pace for days on end. They could march up to 18 miles (30 kilometers) every day. Roman soldiers made temporary camps for overnight stops and moved supplies in carts using horses and oxen.

Roman armies did not let the geography of the land stop them from taking over new lands.

When did the Romans invade Britain?

Julius Caesar was a Roman leader before the start of the Roman Empire. He invaded Britain in 54 BCE. He wanted to stop the Celtic people in Britain from joining forces with people in France and fighting against the Romans. In 43 CE, Emperor Claudius invaded Britain. He was interested in the valuable minerals of the land and also the crops of grain that people were growing. This was the start of over 300 years of Roman rule in Britain.

DID PEOPLE TRY TO RESIST THE ROMANS?

Some groups tried to fight back against the Romans. For example:

- In 60 CE, a woman named Boudicca, queen of the Iceni tribe in Britain, led a violent revolt against the Romans. It took the Romans a year to defeat this attack.
- In Judea in the Middle East, Jews rebelled in 66 CE. The Romans destroyed the holy city of Jerusalem, and the Jews retreated to the mountains. The Romans soon defeated them.

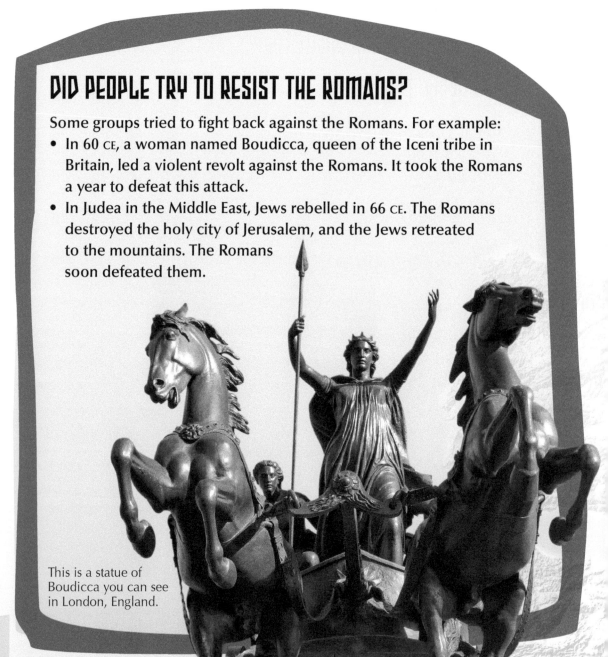

This is a statue of Boudicca you can see in London, England.

This map shows the natural boundaries of the Roman Empire and some of the fortified boundaries (limes) that the Romans created.

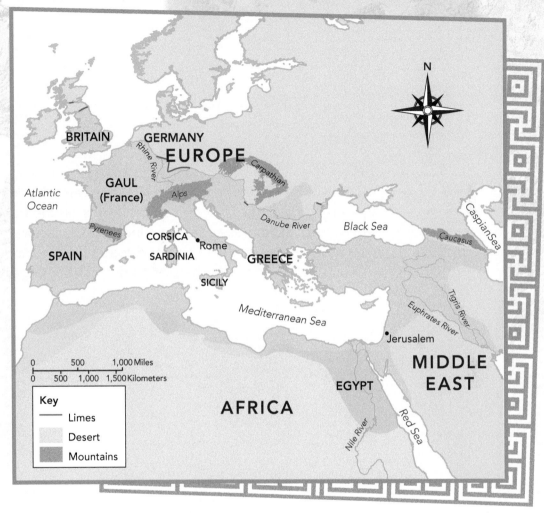

What were the boundaries of the Roman Empire?

The empire had some natural boundaries. The desert areas to the south of North Africa were too hot and dry for the Romans to farm. The Atlantic Ocean to the west of Spain and France was too vast for Roman ships to cross. The Black Sea and large rivers such as the Danube, the Rhine, and the Euphrates were also difficult to cross. Mountains and forests were natural boundaries in some areas, too. However, the Romans managed to cross many natural geographical boundaries. In some areas, they built their own **fortified** boundaries with walls, ditches, forts, and watchtowers. These were called limes.

What was Hadrian's Wall?

After the Romans had invaded Britain, they built Hadrian's Wall. This was a turf and stone wall running for 73 miles (118 kilometers) across northern Britain. This was the northernmost border of the Roman Empire.

Parts of Hadrian's Wall still stand today. It had forts along its length. It was up to 20 feet (6 meters) high and 10 feet (3 meters) wide.

DID YOU KNOW?

There is another Roman wall, north of Hadrian's Wall. It is at the narrowest point of Scotland, between the Firth of Forth and the Firth of Clyde. It is called the Antonine Wall, and it was built by Emperor Antoninus Pius around 142 CE. The land between the Antonine Wall and Hadrian's Wall was never considered part of the Roman Empire, since the Romans never had complete control over it.

The Romans built an elegant town at Caerwent in Wales. The remains of some of the impressive buildings can be seen today.

How did the Romans influence the lands they controlled?

The Romans ruled over a huge area that contained a mix of languages and **cultures**. In some places, such as remote mountainous areas, people's lives did not change much under the Romans. In other areas that were more easily reached, cultures slowly changed to become more Roman. In many places, people spoke Latin (the Romans' language) and began to think of themselves as Romans.

The Romans had a big impact on life in many countries, especially Britain. They built large towns with **amphitheaters**, temples, inns, and bathhouses. They taught British people how to build fine stone buildings and also how to make roads. Many new goods were **imported** to Britain, such as fine pottery and silk.

What Were Travel, Transportation, and Trade Like in the Roman Empire?

The Romans needed excellent **communications** to create and run such a huge empire. Both land and sea travel were important in developing the empire.

Why were roads so important in the empire?

Roman armies needed to be able to march quickly to places to defend the empire. They needed good roads to do this, and to keep army camps at borders supplied with food and weapons. People also used roads for trade and for communicating between the different parts of the empire and Rome. Every new town or city that was captured would have a road that linked to the network leading to Rome. By 200 CE, there were around 53,000 miles (85,000 kilometers) of roads.

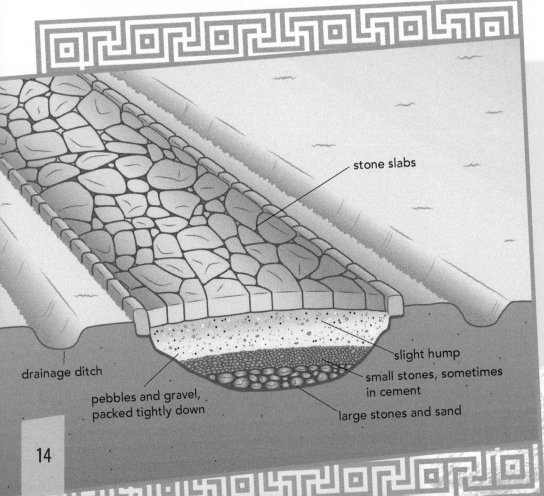

stone slabs

drainage ditch

pebbles and gravel, packed tightly down

slight hump

small stones, sometimes in cement

large stones and sand

This diagram shows how a Roman road was built. The roads were slightly humped in shape, to allow water to drain off to the sides and into ditches.

This is a section of the very first Roman road, the Via Appia. You can see how straight it is.

How did the roads overcome natural obstacles?

Most roads were very straight, taking the shortest possible distance between two points. They would go up and over steep hills instead of going the longer way around. The Romans often did not try to follow the natural **contours** of the land, because they wanted to make roads that allowed the fastest possible travel.

Where mountains were too steep to build straight roads, such as in the Alps, the Romans built curving roads with tight bends up and over the **mountain passes**. They built huge bridges and **viaducts** over rivers and valleys.

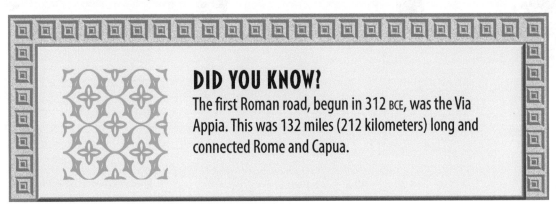

DID YOU KNOW?

The first Roman road, begun in 312 BCE, was the Via Appia. This was 132 miles (212 kilometers) long and connected Rome and Capua.

Did people travel by sea in the Roman Empire?

Romans used sea travel to carry large trade loads. Sea travel was cheaper than overland travel, since large ships could carry more.

Ships were made of wood and had sails and oars. They carried goods such as spices, oil, and grain. They sailed to and from ports across the Mediterranean Sea and the Black Sea. Sea travel was not fast—it took about two or three weeks to sail from Egypt to Rome, for example. Ships taking goods to Rome docked at a seaport called Ostia. The goods would be loaded onto smaller ships and sailed up the Tiber River into Rome.

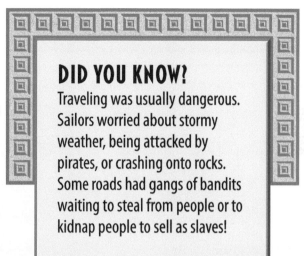

DID YOU KNOW?
Traveling was usually dangerous. Sailors worried about stormy weather, being attacked by pirates, or crashing onto rocks. Some roads had gangs of bandits waiting to steal from people or to kidnap people to sell as slaves!

Roman ships carried containers called amphorae that were full of goods such as wine and olive oil.

How did the weather and the landscape affect sea travel?

There was less sea travel over the winter, when the weather was stormier. Sometimes high winds trapped ships in harbors for weeks at a time. Once at sea, sailors did not have compasses or sea charts. This meant that they preferred to sail in sight of the coast. However, it also meant that many ships were shipwrecked on coastal rocks.

Some sailors **navigated** using the positions of the sun, moon, and stars. They could then sail further from the coast. Some harbors had lighthouses, which also helped sailors to navigate. The Pharos was a huge lighthouse, over 350 feet (110 meters) high, at Alexandria, on the coast of Egypt.

This is how an artist imagined the Pharos might have looked.

What items did Romans trade?

Trade was an important part of the Roman Empire. New goods came from outside of the Roman Empire. Sackloads of silk came from China on the backs of camels, and spices, jewels, and perfumes came from India. Fine glassware and pottery were **exported** out of the empire. The good road network made it easy to transport goods, and the strong navy helped to protect the larger loads carried by ships.

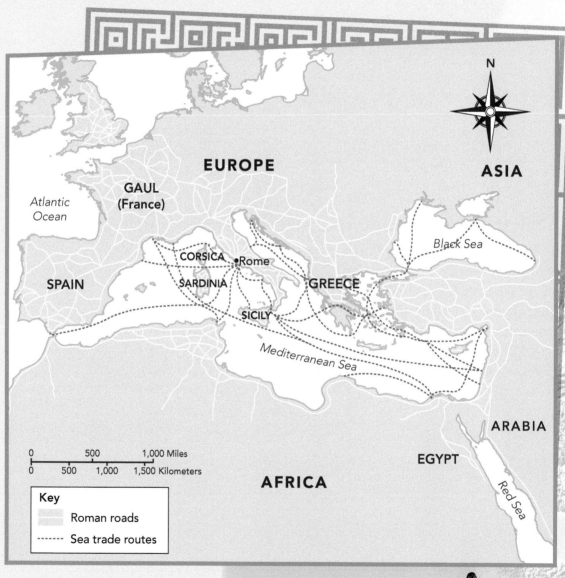

N

EUROPE

ASIA

GAUL
(France)

Atlantic
Ocean

Black Sea

CORSICA

•Rome

SPAIN

SARDINIA

GREECE

SICILY

Mediterranean Sea

| 0 | 500 | 1,000 Miles |
| 0 | 500 | 1,000 | 1,500 Kilometers |

ARABIA

EGYPT

AFRICA

Red Sea

Key

Roman roads

------- Sea trade routes

This map shows the main transportation and trade routes in the Roman Empire.

Traders also sold goods within the empire. Rome and other cities imported lots of food, oil, wine, and wool. Jars of wine were traded out of Italy, France, and Spain, and grain was shipped from Africa. Britain traded its hunting dogs, wool, silver, and lead, while fish sauce, olive oil, and cloth came from Spain. Marble from Greece was used in buildings in the empire.

Did the Romans use money to trade?

During the time of the Roman Empire, people traded goods with coins. There were many coins in use. Different coins had different values and were made of gold, silver, bronze, and copper. The same coins were used throughout the empire, making trading much easier.

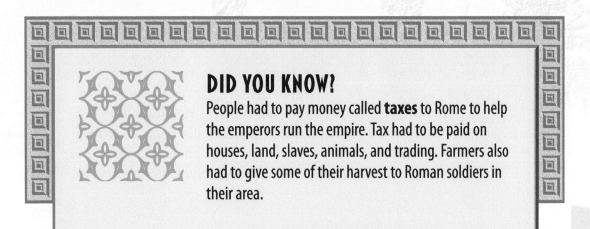

What Were Roman Towns Like?

Some towns and cities already existed at the start of the Roman Empire. Many more were built during the time of the empire. The Romans thought very carefully about town planning.

What was a typical Roman town like?

Some towns began as army camps. Others grew at important travel sites such as crossroads or bridges. Many were set out in a grid pattern, with straight streets running at right angles to each other.

This diagram shows how a typical Roman town was laid out. Many towns followed patterns similar to this.

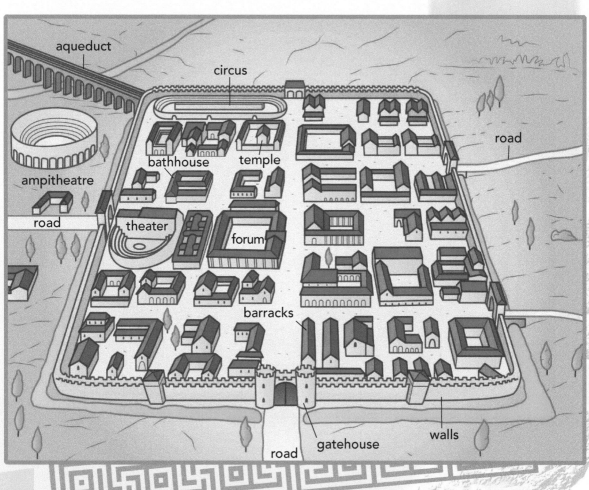

aqueduct

circus

road

bathhouse

temple

ampitheatre

road

theater

forum

barracks

gatehouse

walls

road

Some bathhouses, such as the one in Bath, England, were built on the site of natural **hot springs**. These provided warm water, full of minerals, that people thought were good for their health.

At the main crossroads in a town center there was usually an open space called a **forum**. On market days, the forum would be filled with traders' stalls. Thick stone walls protected towns from attackers. People had to enter through heavy wooden gates in the walls.

Why did Roman towns have bathhouses?

Bathhouses were important places in Roman towns. These were large buildings with lots of different rooms for bathing and washing. There were steam rooms where people could relax, rooms where they could have a massage, and hot and cold pools.

A central heating system called a hypocaust heated the bathhouses. This was a system of pipes that delivered hot air to the floors and walls of the building. Huge **furnaces** in the basement would heat the air and also the water needed for the hot pools.

In some areas, the water had to be delivered from mountain springs into towns. The Romans built amazing lines of pipes, channels, and **aqueducts** to do this. Some were over 25 miles (40 kilometers) long.

What building methods did the Romans use?

One of the most important building methods that the Romans used was the rounded arch. The basic arch shape was used to create other shapes, such as domes and tunnels.

To build an arch, the Romans first built wooden frames in the shape of an arch. They laid stone blocks on top of this. When they dropped in the last block—usually the one in the middle—they could remove the wooden frame. This is because the central block, called the keystone, would balance out the pushing force of the blocks on either side of the arch.

What materials did the Romans use for building?

Some buildings were made of brick and stone. However, this made the walls extremely heavy. The Romans developed a lighter material called **concrete** that solved this problem. They mixed ash with water to make cement, then added sand and small stones to make concrete. It set very hard when it dried. Romans used this concrete to fill the middle of hollow walls. This meant they could build huge buildings that were not in danger of collapsing under their own weight. Important buildings were then faced with stone or marble.

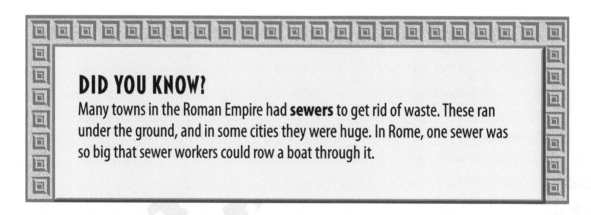

DID YOU KNOW?
Many towns in the Roman Empire had **sewers** to get rid of waste. These ran under the ground, and in some cities they were huge. In Rome, one sewer was so big that sewer workers could row a boat through it.

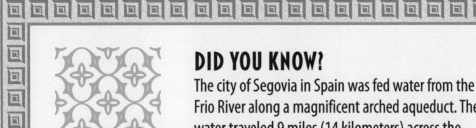

DID YOU KNOW?

The city of Segovia in Spain was fed water from the Frio River along a magnificent arched aqueduct. The water traveled 9 miles (14 kilometers) across the countryside, and the highest part of the aqueduct stands at 93 feet (28.5 meters) above ground. It is one of the best surviving Roman aqueducts. Aqueducts had to flow downhill all the way from the water source to the town, because they relied on gravity alone to move the water.

Were any towns affected by natural disasters?

The huge size of the Roman Empire meant that quite a few towns and cities were affected by **natural disasters**. The most famous natural disaster to take place during Roman times happened in 79 CE. Mount Vesuvius, a volcano in southern Italy, erupted over two days. It buried the town of Pompeii, which lay 6 miles (10 kilometers) south of the volcano, in layers of ash. The town of Herculaneum, to the west of the volcano, was buried under 66 feet (20 meters) of ash and rock.

These are the remains of Pompeii, with Mount Vesuvius in the background. **Archaeologists** have dug through the layers of ash to reach the ruins.

What other disasters happened?

The Tiber River often flooded the city of Rome when there was a lot of rain. The river could rise as much as 50 feet (15 meters) above normal levels. Sometimes parts of the city were underwater for over a week.

In areas around the Aegean Sea, in the eastern part of the Mediterranean, there were often earthquakes. In 365 CE, there was a huge earthquake on the island of Cyprus, which destroyed the town of Kourion.

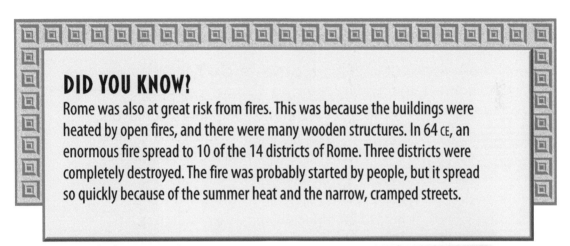

DID YOU KNOW?

Rome was also at great risk from fires. This was because the buildings were heated by open fires, and there were many wooden structures. In 64 CE, an enormous fire spread to 10 of the 14 districts of Rome. Three districts were completely destroyed. The fire was probably started by people, but it spread so quickly because of the summer heat and the narrow, cramped streets.

These are the remains of the Roman town of Kourion.

Lots of land in the Roman Empire was used for farming. Farms produced the food that was needed to feed people in the towns and cities of the empire. They also produced goods for trade. The most valuable crops for trade were grapes, grown to make wine, and olives, grown to make oil.

Some of the farms in the empire were very large. They were owned by wealthy Romans who bought the land from local people. The land was worked by slaves and people employed as farmworkers. The landowners built country houses called **villas** on their farms.

What crops did people grow?

The Roman Empire was huge, and it included many different landscapes. Different areas had different climates, soil types, and **terrain**. This meant that a huge range of crops could be grown, because some crops need different conditions than others. Grapes, olives, and corn were grown in Italy, where the weather was warm. Olives also grew well in Spain. Grain was an important crop in the fertile parts of North Africa, including Egypt. Northern areas, such as Britain and France, had colder weather but good soil. Here, people grew wheat, barley, beans, peas, plums, and apples.

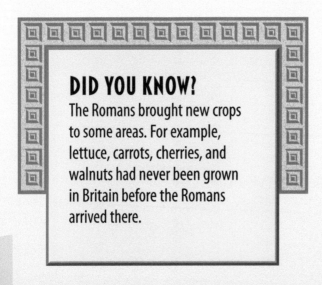

DID YOU KNOW?
The Romans brought new crops to some areas. For example, lettuce, carrots, cherries, and walnuts had never been grown in Britain before the Romans arrived there.

In many areas in the Roman Empire, the soil and climate were ideal for growing valuable crops such as olives.

What took place in the farming year?

The farming year was different across the empire, but certain events took place on most farms. For example, before plowing the fields and planting the seeds, farmers and farmworkers would offer gifts to the gods. They believed this would help their crops to grow well. People celebrated good harvests with sports festivals and large feasts.

What farming methods did the Romans use?

Early Romans harvested grain by hand, using sharp, curved blades called sickles. Later, they invented a harvesting machine called a vallus. A mule or ox would push this through the crop. As the stalks passed over the vallus, a blade cut the grain head off, and it fell into a basket below the blade. This was much quicker than using a sickle. Romans also realized that the soil needed to be tended to. They used animal manure to **fertilize** the soil, and they rotated their crops so that different crops were grown in fields year by year.

Inventions such as the vallus helped the Romans to improve their farming methods and get more from the land.

How else did Romans use the land?

During Roman times, much more land was covered in forest than today. The Romans needed lots of wood for making buildings and ships. They burned smaller pieces of wood for cooking and for heating houses, especially the bathhouses.

Romans plowed fertile farmland to grow crops and grazed cattle on good pastures. On poor, upland slopes, they raised sheep and goats, which were more hardy. On land not used for farming, they often dug quarries and mines for building stone, salt, and valuable minerals such as gold and iron.

How did farming affect the Romans?

Farming was one of the most important industries in the Roman Empire, and it helped to make the empire rich. As new crops and farming methods spread around the empire, farming became more efficient and productive. Landowners of large estates became very wealthy. They showed off their wealth with their luxurious country villas.

There was a huge Roman villa at North Leigh, near Oxford, England. The excellent farmland in the area made the landowners very wealthy.

What Was Roman Society Like?

Life was very different for rich and poor, and for **citizens** and noncitizens. Noncitizens included all women and slaves.

Who ruled in Rome?

The emperor had supreme power. After the first emperor, Augustus Caesar, every emperor had to belong to the same family. This was until Nerva was emperor from 96 to 98 CE. He changed the rules so that every emperor could choose who would rule after him.

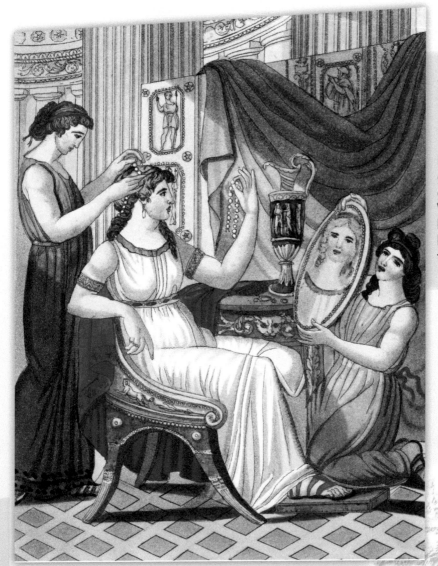

Most Roman girls did not go to school. Wealthy women had maids to help them in their homes.

BECOMING A CITIZEN

In 89 BCE, citizenship was given to any man living in Italy. In 212 CE, every free man living in the empire could become a citizen. However, women and slaves were still excluded.

The lands of the empire were split into areas called **provinces**. A governor ruled each province. The governor was in charge of collecting all the taxes in his province.

What was life like for Roman women?

Roman women had a bit more freedom than in other ancient civilizations, such as ancient Greece. They could leave their homes for shopping and entertainment, to visit bathhouses, and to worship at temples. Some women ran farms and businesses when their husbands were away. But they could not get involved with running the empire, and most did not get educated.

Most rich women did not have jobs. Poorer women had to work, often as maids, farmworkers, spinners, or weavers. Some women were slaves, and a few female slaves became **gladiators**.

Did Roman children go to school?

Most boys went to school. They studied reading, math, Greek, and Latin. Some went on to higher education, which was mostly studying rhetoric. Rhetoric is about speaking well in public, and it was a very important skill for many jobs in the Roman Empire. Some wealthy boys went to Athens to study rhetoric. Poor boys could not get an education.

What jobs did educated Romans do?

Educated Romans could become lawyers, writers, and priests. They could also study to become **architects**, engineers, surveyors, doctors, town planners, and **cartographers**. Artistic Romans were in great demand for the sculptures, paintings, and mosaics that they could produce.

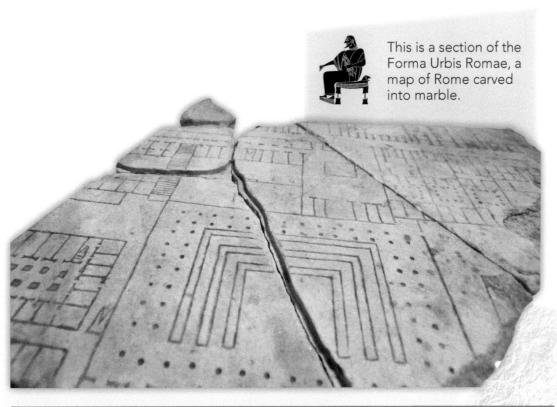

This is a section of the Forma Urbis Romae, a map of Rome carved into marble.

DID YOU KNOW?

Cartography was an important skill in Roman times. Many cities had maps made of them. One example that has survived is the Forma Urbis Romae, a map of the city of Rome, carved into marble slabs. Only fragments of the map have been found, but the completed map would have been huge—59 feet (18 meters) wide and 43 feet (13 meters) tall! It was made to impress people with the size and scale of Rome.

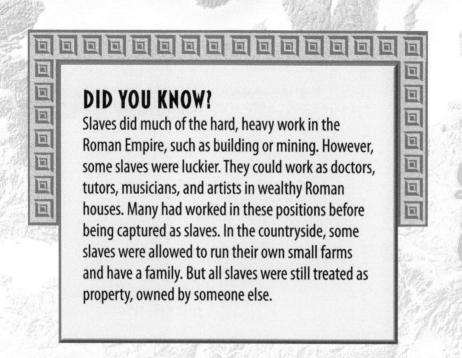

What crafts and trades did Romans learn?

Many Romans were shopkeepers or worked as bakers, butchers, fishmongers, wine sellers, and olive oil sellers. Others had useful craft skills, such as clothes-making, carpentry, pottery, metalworking, glassblowing, and jewelry-making. The wives and children of craftworkers often helped out in the family workshop.

These Roman jewels were found in the ruins of Pompeii.

What did Romans do for fun?

Romans watched plays in theaters built across the empire. Many theaters had a system of ropes that could pull screens across the top, and so shade people from the hot sun. Romans also built amphitheaters. These were round or oval rows of seating with an arena in the center.

The entertainment provided for Romans in the amphitheaters was often very violent. Here they watched slaves called gladiators fight against each other, or wild animals, to the death. Chariot racing was also a very popular Roman sport. Chariot drivers raced teams of horses pulling chariots around a racetrack.

The Colosseum in Rome was a magnificent amphitheater built for a deadly purpose. Its ruins still stand today.

INLAND SEA BATTLES

Sometimes arenas were flooded with water for boats to fight mock sea battles. This made a change from the usual gladiator fights—but still resulted in the deaths of many people.

Was religion important in the Roman Empire?

The religion of the Roman Empire involved gods and goddesses, many of which were based on the ancient Greek gods and goddesses. People could also worship any other gods and goddesses they liked, but they all had to worship the Roman ones.

Christianity spread from Palestine, in the eastern part of the empire, during the first century CE. At first, the Romans did not accept Christianity as a religion, because Christians refused to worship the Roman gods. But Christians believed that Jesus rose from the dead, and so Christianity attracted people with its ideas of everlasting life. The religion gathered more and more followers and went on to become the religion of the Roman Empire in 394 CE.

The Roman religion spread across the whole empire. These are the remains of a Roman temple in Syria.

How Did the Roman Empire Come to an End?

After around 150 CE, people across the empire began to argue about paying taxes to Rome. Taxes had been raised to pay for the army to keep defending the empire. In 166 CE, a **plague** killed many people in the empire. People became angry that they were leading such difficult lives while their leaders in Rome were still spending huge amounts of money on games and races.

Why was the empire split in half?

The years between 235 CE and 284 were very difficult in the empire. Many emperors came to power, but they were then murdered by enemies. There were more plagues, and poor harvests led to **famine**. People had to pay high prices for goods and high taxes. Tribes from the north and the east began attacking the empire.

This Roman coin shows the head of the emperor Diocletian. He split the Roman Empire in two and kept control of the Western Roman Empire for a while.

In 284 CE, when Diocletian became emperor, he realized that the empire was too big to control. So, he split it in two. He took control of the Western Roman Empire, while Maximian became emperor in the Eastern Roman Empire.

Emperor Constantine won many battles as he fought to take control of the empire. This battle was at the Milvian Bridge, which carried a road called the Via Flaminia into Rome.

Did the two halves unite again?

Constantine became emperor of the western empire in 312 CE. From 324 CE, he started reuniting the two halves of the empire, and in 330 CE, he moved the capital from Rome to Byzantium. He renamed the city Constantinople. But the empire was still not strong enough to defend itself from attack.

When did the Roman Empire split again?

In 395 CE, the empire was split into two for good. Honorius moved the western capital from Rome to Ravenna. But the western empire was now under attack from different **barbarian** tribes. These were tribes that came from outside of the Roman Empire. In 410 CE, the Romans abandoned Britain and sent the army to defend other areas. People in other provinces were again weakened by plague and famine, and they did not trust the Roman leaders in Ravenna.

This map shows the two halves of the Roman Empire and the cities they were ruled from. It also shows the routes that the different barbarian tribes took as they brought down the Western Roman Empire.

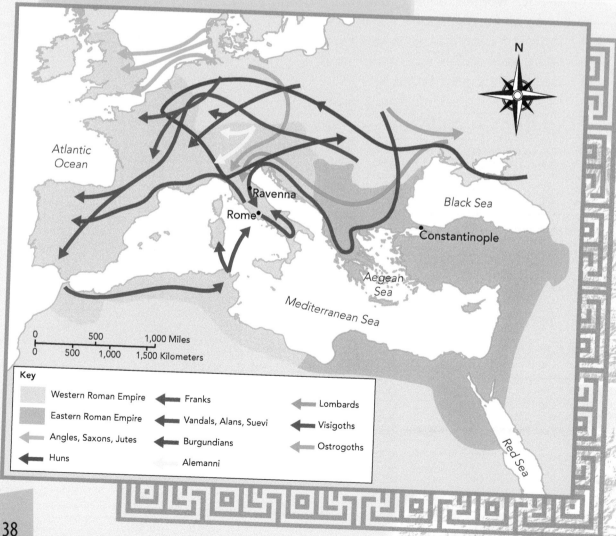

This artist's illustration shows the Vandals destroying the city of Rome. This event weakened Roman rule.

When did the Roman Empire finally collapse?

In 455 CE, a barbarian tribe called the Vandals invaded Italy. For 12 days, they rampaged through Rome. Barbarian generals across the western empire took control of the Roman army. The Roman emperor had almost no power left, and in 476 CE, a barbarian leader declared himself king of Italy. The Western Roman Empire collapsed and split into different barbarian kingdoms. Gradually, the Roman way of life in Europe died out. It continued in the eastern empire, which became known as the Byzantine Empire.

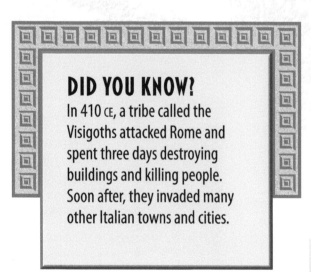

DID YOU KNOW?

In 410 CE, a tribe called the Visigoths attacked Rome and spent three days destroying buildings and killing people. Soon after, they invaded many other Italian towns and cities.

Was Geography Important in Ancient Rome?

The Roman Empire was huge and included many different landscapes. The geography of this large area affected many parts of Roman life, from the crops that they farmed to the borders that they defended.

The location of Rome gave Romans excellent trade links both on land and at sea. Rome was at the center of the empire, and it ruled over all of the Mediterranean coast.

There were excellent communications across the empire, including the road network. This meant that Roman armies could easily push out the empire's borders and could also keep in close contact with the rulers in Rome.

The Alcantara Bridge in Spain is an excellent example of Roman engineering overcoming the landscape.

Many Roman buildings, such as this aqueduct in southern France, still stand today. We can learn about the Romans from these buildings.

Different climates, soils, and terrain across the empire produced a huge range of goods and resources. This helped to increase the wealth and strength of the Roman Empire. Romans adapted to living in different climates. For example, Romans in Britain took to wearing thick socks to keep their feet warm!

Many geographical obstacles stood in the way of Roman progress across the empire. But the Romans developed their skills in building roads, bridges, walls, viaducts, and aqueducts. Most geographical obstacles were eventually overcome. However, even the Romans could not control natural disasters.

Lots of the towns that the Romans built were planned, and many grew in similar ways, all over the empire. Roman culture was spread over a wide geographical area. This is lucky for us, because much of it has been preserved for us to study.

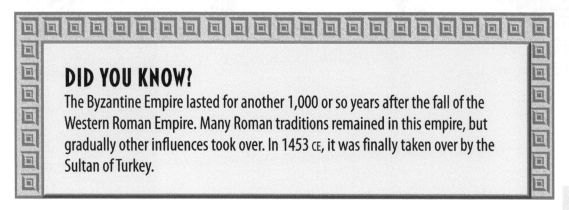

DID YOU KNOW?

The Byzantine Empire lasted for another 1,000 or so years after the fall of the Western Roman Empire. Many Roman traditions remained in this empire, but gradually other influences took over. In 1453 CE, it was finally taken over by the Sultan of Turkey.

Quiz

1

What is the name of the river that flows through Rome?

a) Tiber River

b) Tweed River

c) Achelous River

2

How many hills form the city of Rome?

a) None, it is in a valley

b) Seven

c) Ten

3

Which side of Italy is connected by land to the rest of Europe?

a) The west side

b) The south side

c) The north side

4

What valuable stone did the Romans quarry in Egypt?

a) Green sandstone

b) Red marble

c) Blue granite

5

How many people lived in the Roman Empire?

a) Over 50 million

b) Over 30 million

c) Over 10 million

6

What was the northern border of Roman Britain called?

a) Hadrian's Barrier

b) Hadrian's Gate

c) Hadrian's Wall

7

What is the name of the first Roman road?

a) Via Appia

b) Via Romana

c) Via Ferrata

8

Why did Roman roads have a slightly humped shape?

a) To stop vehicles from traveling too quickly

b) To allow water to drain off into ditches

c) To keep people on the correct side of the road

9

What structures carried water into towns?

a) Viaducts

b) Hypocausts

c) Aqueducts

10

What was the forum in a Roman town?

a) An open space in the center

b) A building where people went to wash and bathe

c) The gate that people passed through into the town

11

What building material did the Romans develop?

a) Asbestos

b) Plasterboard

c) Concrete

12

What was the name of the volcano that buried Pompeii?

a) Mount Olympus

b) Mount Vesuvius

c) Mount Herculaneum

Glossary

amphitheater oval or round building with seats rising in rows from an open, central area

aqueduct channel or pipe built to carry water over a long distance; also the name given to a structure like a bridge for carrying the channel or pipe across a river or valley

archaeologist person who studies objects from history to understand past lives

architect person who designs buildings

barbarian person living outside of the Roman Empire; the Romans believed barbarians were savage and uncivilized

BCE short for "Before the Common Era," relating to dates before the birth of Jesus Christ

cartographer person who creates maps

CE short for the "Common Era," relating to dates after the birth of Jesus Christ

citizen person who is a member of a country or city-state because of being born there or being accepted as a member by law

climate usual weather conditions in a place

communications in geography, communications means the ways of connecting people and includes roads and sea routes as well as exchanging messages

concrete strong, hard building material made of different materials mixed together

contour natural shape and height of the landscape

culture language, ideas, inventions, traditions, and art of a group of people

emperor ruler of an empire

empire group of countries or people ruled over by a powerful leader or government

export take to another country, usually to be sold

famine time when there is not enough food to feed all the people living in an area

fertile able to produce and support plants such as farm crops

fertilize add substances to land to make it more fertile

fortified strengthened to protect against attack

forum central place in Roman towns and cities where people gathered for business and public meetings

furnace equipment for making heat by burning gas, oil, coal, or wood

gladiator person in ancient Rome who fought other people or animals, often to the death, to entertain an audience

hot spring place where naturally warm water emerges from Earth

import bring in from another country, usually to be sold

marble hard, attractive stone that can be cut and polished to a hard, shiny surface

merchant ship ship used for trading goods

mineral substance in Earth that does not come from an animal or a plant

mountain pass lower area of land between two mountain peaks

natural disaster disaster, such as an earthquake, flood, or volcanic eruption, that is caused by nature rather than humans

navigate plan a route and travel by that route

plague disease that spreads quickly and kills many people

plains large, flat area of land

port place where ships load or unload goods

province area of a country or empire that has its own local rulers

sewer pipe or channel that carries away the liquid and solid waste from a town or city

tax money that you pay to a government

terrain natural shape and characteristics of the land

valley long area of low land between mountains or hills

viaduct road or passageway built on a series of arches over a valley or lower routes

villa large, luxurious country house or estate

Find Out More

Books

Hanbury-Murphy, Trudy. *Solving the Mysteries of Ancient Rome* (Digging into History). New York City: Marshall Cavendish Benchmark, 2009.

James, Simon. *Ancient Rome* (Eyewitness). New York City: Dorling Kindersley, 2011.

Macdonald, Fiona. *Ancient Rome* (100 Facts). New York City: Sandy Creek, 2013.

Steele, Philip. *Ancient Rome* (Kingfisher Readers). New York City: Kingfisher, 2012.

Web Sites

FactHound offers a safe, fun way to find Internet sites related to this book. All of the sites on FactHound have been researched by our staff.

Here's all you do:

Visit www.facthound.com

Type in this code: 9781484609644

Places to Visit

The Field Museum, Chicago, Illinois
www.fieldmuseum.org
The Field Museum has an extensive collection of artifacts from
ancient Rome.

Metropolitan Museum of Art, New York
www.metmuseum.org
At the Metropolitan Museum of Art, you can see many examples of
objects and art from ancient Rome.

Tips For Further Research
Seven hills of Rome
See if you can find out the names of the seven hills of Rome. In modern
Rome, what buildings are at the tops of the seven hills?

Climate extremes
The Roman Empire was huge and stretched from Britain in the north to
Egypt in the south. Think about how different the climates are in these
places. Do some research to compare the climates in these two countries
today—average temperatures and average rainfall, for example. See if you
can find out where might have been the hottest, driest, wettest, windiest,
and coldest places in all of the Roman Empire.

Index